Habit to Heart

Praying Real Prayers to a Prayer-Loving God

Sharon Norris Elliott

Published by G8 Press (n.\gāt pres\)
P.O. Box 9043
Cedarpines Park, CA 92322-9043
www.G8press.com

Table of Contents

ॐॐ

Pray

Day 1

For the most part, we don't ask for prayer until we're desperate – at the end of our rope. We try to do everything in our power to solve the problem, work out the issue, smooth over a misunderstanding, and medicate the illness. When we finally decide there is nothing more we can do, we pray. That's why when people ask me to pray for them, I take it seriously. They have come to the end of themselves and they are now rallying the troops to bombard Heaven with their desperate request.

I'm guilty too of being more self-sufficient than I should be. Paul tells the Colossians, "Continue earnestly in prayer, being vigilant in it with thanksgiving" (Col 4:2 NKJ). Instead of waiting until we've spun our wheels, lost sleep, and maybe even spent lots of money, why not pray. If we "continue earnestly in prayer," when troubles arise, we'll already be in conversation with God. We can just keep talking with Him, turning our problems over to Him, and thanking Him even in advance of actually seeing the answers.

Try getting into the practice of praying first. Dedicate yourself this month to setting aside a special time every day to pray. Don't know what to pray? Try this simple formula. Use the word A.C.T.S. to help you get into the act of praying.

- **A**doration: Open your time of prayer by adoring God. Talk to Him about how great He is. Still stumped? Start by taking a letter of the alphabet each day and think of words that describe God. Then adore Him by telling Him how much you appreciate that attribute about Him. Today, use the letter "A" and tell God, "Father, you are awesome, able, and attentive." Lavish Him with praise about how He manifests Himself to you in these ways. Tomorrow, use the letter "B" and tell God, for example, that you've noticed how big, beautiful, and full of blessings He is. You'll cover at least 26 days this way. By the end of the alphabet, you will have caught on to this adoration thing.

- **C**onfession: You probably won't have much trouble with this part of prayer. Confession is merely agreeing with God about the sinful things we've done or thought. Might as well own up, He knows all about it anyway. Spend the next portion of your prayer time confessing to God.

- **T**hanksgiving: Next, spend some time thanking God. You might want to start by thanking Him for the simple fact that you're in the right mind to even remember to pray. Enumerate to God everything for which you are thankful.

- **S**upplication: Probably the easiest of all is supplication. Here's the part of prayer in which you ask God for whatever you need. Many times, we begin with supplication, but notice that in this acronym, supplication is last. After we've spent time adoring Him, confessing our sins, and thanking Him for His goodness, our supplications are then properly shaped.

Day 1: Pray

- Decide upon your daily prayer time.
- Decide upon a special place for your prayer time.
- Pray.

Adoration:

Confession:

Day 1: Pray (continued)

Thanksgiving:

Supplication:

Ask

Day 2

Ry Cooder wrote a traditional gospel chorus that says, "Jesus is on the main line, tell Him what you want. Call Him up and tell Him what you want." This song was written back in the days when there were such things as "main lines" and "party lines" on the telephone. You received your major messages via the main line, but every now and then, you could get hooked into a party line, a slip-up when multiple customers were connected to the same phone line. You can imagine the confusion that could ensue if several conversations were going on at the same time. Cooder's song points out that you can talk directly to Jesus with no interference, having His complete attention when asking for what you need.

The blind man on the Jericho road found out about the main line to Jesus. Here's the account:

> "Then it happened, as He was coming near Jericho, that a certain blind man sat by the road begging. And hearing a multitude passing by, he asked what it meant. So they told him that Jesus of Nazareth was passing by. And he cried out, saying, 'Jesus, Son of David, have mercy on me!' ...So Jesus stood still and commanded him to be brought to Him. And when he had come near, He asked him, saying, 'What do you want Me to do for you?' And he said, 'Lord, that I may receive my sight.' Then Jesus said to him, 'Receive your sight; your faith has made you well.' And immediately he received his sight, and followed Him, glorifying God. And all the people, when they saw it, gave praise to God" (Luke 18:35-43 NKJ).

5

It's a simple story with such a profound lesson for us. We make prayer so complicated when it's really quite the opposite. Here are our lessons on prayer from this narrative:

1. **Be where Jesus is.** This man sat on the same road where Jesus walked. Ask Him on which road you need to travel, in order to hear His answer to your prayer. Be in sync.

2. **Ask for mercy.** Mercy is *not* getting what we do deserve. Involve confession in our times of prayer. Realize there will need to be a turning from ways that are not pleasing to Him.

3. **Make specific requests.** Be explicit and unambiguous with what we're asking Jesus to do or supply. Looking Jesus in the face with our requests will temper what we ask of Him. We're liable not to ask for trivial things.

4. **Accept Jesus' answer by faith.** God delights in answering the prayers of the saints. Accept His answer.

5. **Immediately operate in the answer.** Instantly begin operating in the new way. If we couldn't see before, we now should walk like we can see. If we were broke before, we now should operate like people with good financial sense.

6. **Follow Jesus in the strength of that answered prayer.** Let's embrace our blessings and use our answered prayers to be even better Christians.

7. **Glorify God.** Give God His props for the answer to our prayers.

8. **Let people see what God has done.** Testify. Let others know what God has done.

Call Him and tell Him your needs. Prayer is not hard work. Try it.

Day 2: Ask

Today, journal your personal responses or reactions to the eight points of this devotion. For example, in the section "Be where Jesus is," you might write something like, "Lord, I want to be on the road you are on as I travel through my marriage. What "street" should I be on and which direction should I go?" Journal through the rest of the points with your personal feedback.

1. Be where Jesus is.

2. Ask for mercy.

3. Make specific requests.

4. Accept Jesus' answer by faith.

5. Immediately operate in the answer.

6. **Follow Jesus in the strength of that answered prayer.**

7. **Glorify God.**

8. **Let people see what God has done.**

Build an Altar
Day 3

During King David's reign, the tabernacle (the movable tent) that Moses had made was erected at the high place in Gibeon. This tabernacle represented the presence of God among the people. At one particular time when David sinned, he needed a more immediate and convenient altar, so God sent him to a man named Ornan and instructed David to build on Ornan's threshing floor.
1 Chronicles 21:26 says, "And David built there an altar to the LORD, and offered burnt offerings and peace offerings, and called on the LORD; and He answered him from heaven by fire on the altar of burnt offering."

Thanks to Jesus, the sacrificial system is out, the need to go through Levitical priests to get to God is out, and the need to stand before a particular altar whenever we pray is out. However, even though all those things are out, the spirit of each part of David's worship is still in. You see, my body is now the temple (see I Cor 6:19), and it's my responsibility to build an altar to the Lord in my heart, maintain it, and visit it frequently. I take my sin, shame and sorrow to God at this altar and offer them as I would a burnt offering, letting God's fire consume them and reprove me. I take my confidences, joys, and praise as peace offerings, willing to share them with my Master and continue to submit them to Him. I call on the Lord at my altar, discuss my requests and desires with Him, and seek His face.

Finally, it is at the altar where God answers from Heaven by fire. Since my body is the temple, I can never leave my altar. As I maintain altar-consciousness and listen for God's voice, I will hear Him speak through His Word, through other Christian brothers and sisters, and even through observations of nature, which after all is the work of His hands.

11

Consider these two verses:

- "...For we are the temple of the living God. As God has said: 'I will live with them and walk among them, and I will be their God, and they will be my people'" (2 Cor 6:16 NIV).

- "You also, like living stones, are being built into a spiritual house to be a holy priesthood, offering spiritual sacrifices acceptable to God through Jesus Christ" (1 Pet 2:5 NIV).

Become altar-conscious. If you're just starting out, build your heart's altar to the Lord by making a determination to spend daily time with Him. You may have to repair your neglected altar. That's alright; just do it and take up where you left off. If you already spend regular times with God, keep it up. Whatever the case, it's a joy to know that God eagerly desires to spend time with us.

As you are altar-conscious today, take part in the three altar-actions in which David participated.

First, take your sin offering to God, as a burnt offering and let God's fire consume it and reprove you.

Day 3: Build an Altar

Now take your confidences, joys, and praise to God as peace offerings, willingly sharing them with Him and submitting them to Him.

Day 3: Build an Altar

Now call on the Lord in the altar of your heart and discuss your requests and desires with Him, seeking His face concerning them.

But I Give Myself to Prayer
Day 4

By nature, I am a doer. I'm not one to sit around waiting for things to happen. If nothing is going on, I tend to find something to do. I guess I believe the old English proverb by H.G. Bohn that says, "An idle brain is the devil's workshop." Taking the ramifications of this saying to its natural conclusion, I should involve my mind with thoughts worth thinking. Then, if a healthy and holy thought is worth thinking, the idea is worth acting upon. Thus I get to my tendency to make things happen or to find something to do.

The Bible speaks to diligence in work as well. Take a look at these verses:

- "Make it your ambition to lead a quiet life, to mind your own business and to work with your hands…"
  (1 Thes 4:11 NIV).

- "Never be lacking in zeal, but keep your spiritual fervor, serving the Lord" (Rom 12:11 NIV).

- "He who has been stealing must steal no longer, but must work, doing something useful with his own hands, that he may have something to share with those in need"
  (Eph 4:28 NIV).

- "Our people must learn to devote themselves to doing what is good, in order that they may provide for daily necessities and not live unproductive lives"
  (Titus 3:14 NIV).

God expects us to be busy, but we mustn't just come up with ideas of what we ought to be doing. Six little words in Psalm 109 show us where to start. "But I give myself to prayer" (Ps 109:4b NKJ). The only way to be sure we are doing what we should be doing is to stop long enough to get direction from God.

So today, before charging into your activities full speed ahead, stop. Ask God what He would have the doer in you to do. Now here's the hard part; wait until you get an answer. Take a few minutes to read from the Bible – maybe try a passage from Psalms or Proverbs – and reflect upon what God says to you. Thank God for the time spent together and ask Him to come along with you for the rest of the day. You may be surprised by how your words and actions are tempered when God's presence and guidance is with you every step.

Let's adopt as one of our life verses, "But I give myself to prayer." Oh my, how all that we do will be miraculously transformed!

Journal here your to-do list for today.

Before charging full speed into your activities, stop. Ask God what He would have the doer in you to do. Now wait for His answer.

Day 4: But I Give Myself to Prayer

Now journal your thanks to God for the time you've spent together and ask Him to come along for the rest of the day.

I Choose to Hear

Day 5

A gorgeous Christian Conference center on the East coast is located right on the banks of the Chesapeake Bay. Although all of the rooms are cozy, if you're lucky, you can spend your stay in a coveted room with a bay view. During my last visit, however, I was not assigned one of those rooms. Instead, my view looked out on the pool, yes a body of water, but it's not the Chesapeake Bay, especially at sunset. Besides that, my room was the first one off the center lobby, just behind the elevators, and on the main hallway that led to the dining area. Ever so often, I could hear the little "ding" as the elevator doors open and closed, and could pick up snatches of laughter and conversation as folks headed to meals.

At first, I thought if it were possible, it would be nice to shift to the other side of the inn and another hallway where I'd be able to enjoy the bay view and a little more quiet. But then I discovered something. I had a strong internet signal in my room. Generally, the internet signal can only be picked up in the center lobbies and the business center. If you want to log on, you have to take your computer to those areas. So now my choice: do I lug all my unpacked stuff across the hall to enjoy the view, or do I kick off my shoes, put on my jammies, and log on whenever I want?

My choice was not just about the view of the bay or the pool. My choice concerned which was more valuable to me: seeing or hearing. If I stayed in my current room, I'd have to leave it (which would require the work of looking at least slightly presentable) to sit in a public area anytime I wanted to enjoy the bay view. If I moved, I'd be inconvenienced whenever I chose to hear from friends or communicate with them via the internet.

Would I rather see God or hear God? Obviously I want to do both, but if I had to make the choice, I'd rather hear Him. This room dilemma caused me to realize just how much I value the sound of God's voice as it rings in my heart and mind. It's God's voice that spoke to the writers of the Scriptures I love so much – those words which form the backdrop for my very profession as a minister of God's word as I write and teach.

God's voice is His word, and even when we can't see Him in the circumstances, what a comfort to know we can hear His voice. John 10:27 says, "My sheep hear My voice, and I know them, and they follow Me" (NKJ). Wherever we might be placed, may we always be able to "connect" with God's voice and clearly hear His messages to us.

Listening is as much a part of prayer as is talking. Instead of talking today, as much as possible, simply listen. Go through the day with a God-consciousness. As you hear or observe things, think in your heart, "God, what do you think about that?" Then listen for His voice with the ears of your spirit. Journal here what He has to say.

Day 5: I Choose to Hear (continued)

Intercessory Expectation
Day 6

Has anyone ever asked you to pray for them? Did you do it? It's one thing to pray for your friends, but quite another to pray and really expect something to happen.

In Acts chapter 12, Peter is thrown in jail and Herod's intention was to kill him after the Passover. Verse 5 tells us, "Peter was therefore kept in prison, but constant prayer was offered to God for him by the church" (NKJ). The night before Peter was to be taken back before Herod, he was not even fretting. Even though he was chained, his coat and shoes were off and he was sleeping. When an angel showed up to miraculously deliver him, the angel had to shake him awake and tell him to get dressed. Peter was led right past the guards, through the iron gate of the city, and down the streets to freedom.

The funny part happened when he got to the house where the believers were gathered praying for his release. The passage takes up the story:

- "...he came to the house...where many were gathered together praying. And as Peter knocked at the door of the gate, a girl named Rhoda came to answer. When she recognized Peter's voice, because of her gladness she did not open the gate, but ran in and announced that Peter stood before the gate. But they said to her, 'You are beside yourself...It is his angel.' Now Peter continued knocking; and when they opened the door and saw him, they were astonished" (Acts 12:12-16 NKJ).

Why were they astonished? Wasn't this what they were praying for?

Intercession is the act of pleading on behalf of another. We need to develop a sense of intercessory expectation. When we say we'll pray for someone, we should not be just giving lip service. We are taking on the responsibility to carry that load for them until something happens. And we need to expect that God will come through. Peter wasn't worried; the saints were praying and prayer is a powerful thing. They should have been expecting God's answer.

James 5:16 says, "Therefore confess your sins to each other and pray for each other so that you may be healed. The prayer of a righteous man is powerful and effective" (NIV).

Take it seriously when someone asks you to pray for them and then follow-up, expecting to rejoice in God's perfect answers.

For whom are you praying? Has anyone asked you to specifically pray for them? Journal here your prayers for others. Indicate your positive expectation that God will indeed respond to your need.

Day 6: Intercessory Expectation

Day 6: Intercessory Expectation (continued)

On Approaching God
Day 7

Using my computer and a program called Skype®, I can call my sons (and anyone else who has Skype) and see them as we talk. With just a few clicks, I visited with Mark who is thousands of miles away at college, saw his room, and "met" his roommates. Then I visited with Matthew while he ate his bowtie pasta meal. All of us had the same thing in mind: let's call each other and talk. Skype erased the miles and allowed us to be together for a few moments.

Prayer is like Skype. Prayer is the program that erases the miles between Heaven and earth and ushers us into the presence of God. Through prayer, we meet Him face-to-face and have conversation. We talk and He listens; He talks and we listen. We respond back and forth. When we have the program—connect with God through Jesus Christ—we can approach God.

However, I wouldn't want to use Skype and have my boys see me if I looked bad. Each time I visit with them using this program, I want to be presentable. As with Skype, so with prayer. I'm not saying we only pray when we're in great shape and nothing's wrong; I'm saying we ought to approach God regarding Him with respect. Aaron's sons didn't do this and were severely punished. Leviticus 10:1-2 says, "Then Nadab and Abihu, the sons of Aaron, each took his censer and put fire in it, put incense on it, and offered profane fire before the LORD, which He had not commanded them. So fire went out from the LORD and devoured them, and they died before the LORD" (NKJ).

God explained His actions. "By those who come near Me I must be regarded as holy; and before all the people I must be glorified" (Lev 10:3 NKJ). We are welcome to approach Him, but we must remember to do so with the proper respect for who He is. God lays forth two requirements here for approaching Him. He says, "I must be regarded as holy," and "I must be glorified." Matthew Henry's commentary explains it this way.

> What was it that God spoke? "I will be sanctified in those that come nigh me, whoever they are, and before all the people I will be glorified" (KJV).
> - Note, First, Whenever we worship God, we come nigh unto him, as spiritual priests. This consideration ought to make us very reverent and serious in all acts of devotion, that in them we approach God, and present ourselves before him.
> - Secondly, It concerns us all, when we come nigh to God, to sanctify him, that is, to give him the praise of his holiness, to perform every religious exercise as those who believe that the God we serve is a holy God, a God of spotless purity and transcendent perfection, <Isa. 8:13>.
> - Thirdly, when we sanctify God we glorify him, for his holiness is his glory; and, when we sanctify him in our solemn assemblies, we glorify him before all the people, confessing our own belief of his glory and desiring that others also may be affected with it.
> - Fourthly, if God be not sanctified and glorified by us, he will be sanctified and glorified upon us. He will take vengeance on those that profane his sacred name by trifling with him. If his rent be not paid, it shall be distrained for.

Bottom line: As the gospel song says, "Call Him up and tell Him what you want." Approach God often, but approach God right.

Day 7: On Approaching God

Write your prayer to God about His holiness. Discuss with Him the manner in which you approach Him. Listen as He reveals any ways in which you limit your access to Him.

Day 7: On Approaching God (continued)

On Calming Storms
Day 8

Scott Krippayne recorded an amazing song entitled *Sometimes He Calms The Storm*. The lyrics alert us to the proper perspective we need to have about the troubles that pass through our lives. In a nutshell, the song says that God can stop our storms, and sometimes He decides to do that. However, there are times when He allows the storms to continue all around us and instead of stopping the wind and waves, He chooses to calm us.

When Peter walked on water, he wasn't walking on the smooth surface of a calm sea. He strode to Jesus on boisterous waves. Wind whipped around, wreaked havoc with his hair and threatened to blow the tunic right off his back. Yet, Peter walked on, he stayed on top of the waves as long as his eyes were on Jesus.

It's the nature of a storm to cause devastation. We can expect a certain amount of fallout; it just doesn't have to be us who fall out. Jesus eventually did calm the storm Peter was experiencing, but not until He had calmed Peter. And what calmed Peter? The simple knowledge that Jesus was there on the waves.

Psalm 107:29-30 says, "He calms the storm, so that its waves are still. Then they are glad because they are quiet; so He guides them to their desired haven" (NKJ). Our inner storms matter most to our Lord because we matter so much to Him. External circumstances run a distant second to His concern about the condition of our hearts.

Turn your attention today away from the storm raging around you. Focus on Jesus and Jesus alone. He will direct you as to how to walk on the waves. Before you know it, either the waves won't matter to you anymore, or the storm will have passed. Either way, you'll still be afloat.

Day 8: On Calming Storms

Pray about a specific storm you are facing. Listen for His direction on how to walk toward Him on the waves.

Day 8: On Calming Storms (continued)

Our Vows
Day 9

We use our words much too loosely and thoughtlessly. I cringe when I hear people evoke God's name in their fits of rage. Besides the blatantly blasphemous outcry of the name of Jesus to show frustration, or attaching God's name to a curse word, I'm particularly offended when someone declares, "I swear to God," and then continue by asserting what he/she will or won't do.

The words of our mouths are important, especially when we make vows to God. Ecclesiastes 5:4-5 says, "When you make a vow to God, do not delay to pay it; for He has no pleasure in fools. Pay what you have vowed—Better not to vow than to vow and not pay" (NKJ).

What vows have you made to God?
- To stop smoking, overeat, drink in excess, or fornicate.
- To start exercising, drink more water, eliminate salt.
- To read my Bible every day.
- To pray diligently.
- To be a better husband, wife, father, mother, son, daughter, student, employee, or church member.
- To tithe regularly.
- God, if you just get me out of this one I'll...

God says we are fools when we make vows to Him and then don't follow through. Why? Because He's true to His word. When we call on Him in a vow, He starts to move in our direction to assist us. He puts things in motion in the heavenly realm to bring about the blessings associated with the carrying out of those vows. For example:
- When we seek God for help by vowing to turn away from evil, God starts the health machine because He says, "Do

not be wise in your own eyes; fear the LORD and depart from evil. It will be health to your flesh, and strength to your bones" (Prov 3:7-8 NKJ).

- When we vow to read our Bibles regularly, God starts to send stronger faith our way because "…faith comes by hearing, and hearing by the word of God" (Rom 10:17 NKJ).
- And when we vow to tithe, God starts binding up that which would seek to destroy us as He indicates when He says, "Bring all the tithes into the storehouse… And I will rebuke the devourer for your sakes, so that he will not destroy the fruit of your ground, nor shall the vine fail to bear fruit for you in the field..." (Mal 3:10-11 NKJ).

You see, God's not like us. He actually takes us at our word (contrary to how we don't take Him at His). Therefore, when we renege on our vows, we throw a wrench in the works of the very machine that already started to manufacture blessings for us. Foolish!

Let's only make a vow when we mean it. And the next time we feel the need to make a vow to God, remember the seriousness of what we are saying, and the lengths God Himself will go to in order to help us see it through. This knowledge should spur us on to successfully fulfill that vow, and engender a heart of gratefulness to God.

Day 9: On Calming Storms

Have you made any vows to God lately? If so, what were they? Is your vow rash or reasonable? Journal here about your vow(s) and how you plan to trust God to help you fulfill it/them.

If not, journal here about your appreciation of feeling so secure in God that there's no need to make vows.

Day 9: On Calming Storms (continued)

Paul's Prayer, Our Path
Day 10

Paul prays over the saints in Colossians1:9-12. First he says he does not cease to pray for them (verse 9a), which indicates his love and dedication. Then the prayer sets up a six-point goal to which believers everywhere should attain.

- Point 1: "that you may be *filled* with the knowledge of His will in all wisdom and spiritual understanding…"

The Greek word for "filled" here comes from a word that literally means "to cram." Remember when you crammed for exams in school? We had to get that information into our heads because it was vital for us to pass the upcoming test. What are we doing to cram in the knowledge of God's will? Are we as preoccupied with the desire to fulfill His will as we were with passing that history class? In order to be "filled with the knowledge of His will," we need to be about the business of cramming His Word into our spirits and lives. Only by knowing His Word, will we know His will, and understand what He wants us to do.

- Point 2: "…that you may have a *walk worthy* of the Lord, fully pleasing Him…"

Walking worthy means to be occupied appropriately. Are we conducting ourselves in a manner that would please our Master? God expects us to act a certain way in order to draw people to Himself through us.

- Point 3: "…*being fruitful* in every good work…"

Are we fertile, fruit-bearing believers? In other words, will our good works nourish others? Is anyone able to pluck from us that which will bring them closer to the Lord? Fruit trees don't bear fruit to nourish themselves. The works of our hands should be beneficial for someone else.

- Point 4: "…and *increasing* in the knowledge of God…"

What is something new you have learned about God in the past week? Our relationship with God will remain vibrant as we learn more and more about Him. There are infinite things to know about our infinite God. The more we know about Him, the more we'll love and appreciate Him, and the more precious will be our relationship with Him. (Make a list of what you know about God and then ask God to add something new to the list – a new understanding of who He is – at least once a month.)

- Point 5: "...*strengthened* with all might, according to His glorious power, for all patience and longsuffering with joy..."

In order to accomplish living a life in which we walk worthy, are fruitful and increasing in the knowledge of God, Paul knew we'd need some extra-special strength. He prayed that we'd be enabled with the ability of God to have hopeful endurance, fortitude, and calm delight as we carry out our call to live this way. What a joy to know we're not expected to live for God in our own power! God gives us the job description and then the strength to pull it off.

- Point 6: "...*giving thanks* to the Father who has qualified us to be partakers of the inheritance of the saints in the light."

Let's not get so caught up in doing Christian work that we forget to express gratitude because God has qualified us to share in all He has in store for His saints.

If we spend our time in pursuit of (being filled with) the knowledge of His will (Lord, what would you have me to do?); walking in a worthy fashion; being fruitful in every good work God's called us to do; increasing in the knowledge of Him (getting to know Him better); operating in His strength; and giving Him thanks; we'll be living as we should. Take Paul's prayer and personalize it. Watch your Christian life flourish.

Dear God, fill me with the knowledge of Your will. Let me know, without a doubt, what You want me to do. Guide my footsteps so that my walk is worthy and pleasing to You. Allow the good works of my hands to be nourishment for others. Reveal Yourself to me in new ways so that I may know You better. Help me to relax in Your strength to live this life as I should. Thank you for bringing me in, giving me a place on Your team, and assuring me of the prize at the end. Amen.

(Colossians passage is quoted from the New King James version, italics added.)

Day 10: Paul's Prayer; Our Path

In your own words and according to your own present life situation, pray each segment of Paul's prayer. The following phrases will help you get started.

- *Filled* with the knowledge of His will

Day 10: Paul's Prayer; Our Path

- Have a **walk worthy** of the Lord

- *Fruitful* in every good work

- *Increasing* in the knowledge of God

Day 10: Paul's Prayer; Our Path (continued)

- ***Strengthened*** with all might

- ***Giving thanks*** to the Father

Pray for an Open Door
Day 11

Lots of people go to church regularly without a second thought given to how the church really functions. Services start every Sunday at the same time. The doors are open, the lights are on, the instruments and musicians are ready, the choir and ushers are in place. We expect our bulletin to list the current activities, and we expect the Power Point slides to accurately show us the words of the praise songs and the outline of the message. Things just happen, right?

Obviously, many people are behind the scenes to pull that worship service off without a hitch. And all the elements involved are supposed to work together to bring us to the expectant moment – the preaching of the Word of God. After all is said and done – after the responsive reading and praise songs have allowed us to participate in the worship, after the choir has excited us, after the announcements have interested us, after the offering has allowed us to contribute our gifts – we're at church to hear from God.

Are we praying for an open door for the Word? The apostle Paul asked for just such a thing. Colossians 4:3-4 says, "Meanwhile praying also for us, that God would open to us a door for the word, to speak the mystery of Christ, for which I am also in chains, that I may make it manifest, as I ought to speak" (NKJ).

The ultimate reason for our attendance at church (and at other Christian events like retreats and conferences) is to hear the Word of God from His preachers. Let's be diligent to pray for those who preach the Word. They are preaching the mystery of Christ and they need open doors to reach who they should reach, and His anointing to make the message clear.

Day 11: Pray for an Open Door

Journal your prayers about those who preach and teach the Word to you.

Day 11: Pray for an Open Door (continued)

Pray for Me

Day 12

As Paul was closing out his letter to the church at Rome, he embarked upon a conversation about his upcoming itinerary. He tells his readers that he is going to Jerusalem to take the believers there a contribution from the Gentile Christians in Macedonia and Achaia. Paul knows, however, that there are folks in and around Judea who have it in for him. So, if he plans to get to Rome after visiting Jerusalem, he'll need somebody to have his back. Thus he writes to the Romans, "Now I beg you, brethren, through the Lord Jesus Christ, and through the love of the Spirit, that you strive together with me in prayers to God for me" (Rom 15:30 NKJ).

Paul was serious. He says, "I beg (beseech) you…strive together with me in prayers to God for me." Let's break down this request.
* To beg or beseech means "to call near, invoke, and implore."
* Paul referred to the Romans as brethren and the word he used comes from a Greek word meaning "a brother from the womb."
* Paul asked for the Romans to "sunagonizomai." To strive together means to struggle in company with and to be a partner or assistant.
* Then Paul asked for the prayers to be "to God" and "for me." He was only interested in having people go *to God* on his behalf. Those who didn't know God need not apply. Thinking good thoughts wasn't good enough. He also wanted to be sure they knew they were praying specifically *for him*.

These are the conditions when someone says, "Pray for me." They have reached the point of begging for something and realize that every other means has been expended. They know they're in for a fight, so reinforcements are gathered. It's obvious they won't be able to face the situation alone and need "family" members who can identify and who care enough to be there.

They don't need people to play around or forget when they are in a fix and need help.

Let's not throw this request around nor take it lightly. Recognize the serious nature of the simple appeal, "Pray for me." Don't ask others unless you're serious. And the next time someone asks you, go in earnest to the heavenly throne room. Pour out their requests before God as if they were your own. You are striving together. If she goes down, you go down. If she overcomes, you overcome.

Day 12: Pray for Me

Take special time today to pray for others – those who have asked you to pray for them. If no one has asked you to pray them, look at Ephesians 6:19 and pray for your leaders.

Day 12: Pray for Me (continued)

Praying for the Next Generation
Day 13

I wrote the book *Raising Boys to be like Jesus* because I truly believe that boys like Jesus become men of God. In the rearing of my own boys, I did my best to use each and every one of the principles in the book gleaned from the life of Jesus. However, I knew I could pour Jesus into my boys while they lived in my house, it is still up to them to place a stopper in their own spirit so that He won't drain out. They must come to a point at which Jesus – and all the lessons we taught and lived before them – matters personally to them. Now that they are grown, the best I can do is pray.

I feel King David's heart on this same issue. He had reached the end of his life and he was turning the kingdom over to his son Solomon. David had made all the preparations for building the temple, laid out the plans on paper (or on whatever they wrote on in those days), chosen the artisans, and gathered the gold, silver and precious stones into storehouses ready to go. He admonished the people to remain true to the Lord and then he turned his attention to praying for his son. David prayed, "And give my son Solomon a loyal heart to keep Your commandments and Your testimonies and Your statutes, to do all these things, and to build the temple for which I have made provision" (1 Chron 29:19 NKJ).

You may not have children of your own, but you can join in praying this prayer for the next generation. Pray sincerely that the Lord would give our children a loyal heart to keep God's commandments, God's testimonies, and God's statutes. Pray that they would do all the things God requires of them. And pray that they build on the spiritual heritage we have made for them.

53

Although they are not perfect, I am thankful to be able to say so far, so good with my boys. Let's put this prayer into action for all our kids and grandkids, boys and girls, to raise up our next generation of mighty men and women of God.

Day 13: Praying for the Next Generation

Journal your prayers for all the children in your life.

Day 13: Praying for the Next Generation (continued)

Praying to our Triune God
Day 14

Whenever we try to explain God, all we have is earthly examples and the limits of language. An infinite God can hardly be adequately explained by the finite, but that's all we have to work with and the best we can do. Recently, when I was asked a question about prayer and the Trinity, I found myself in this infinite-God-finite-language dilemma. The question was: to whom are we praying: God the Father, God the Son Jesus, or God the Holy Spirit?

First of all, we needed to establish a clear understanding of the Trinity. How is God one yet three? The best explanation I have ever heard was from Dr. Fred Campbell. Think of the sun in the sky.

- The sun has mass; it is a thing that exists. The mass represents God the Father. God told Moses, "I AM WHO I AM... Thus you shall say to the children of Israel, 'I AM has sent me to you'" (Ex 3:14 NKJ).
- The sun gives off light. The light represents God the Son, Jesus Christ. Light shows us the way to God. Jesus Himself says, "I am the way, the truth, and the life. No one comes to the Father except through Me" (Jn 14:6 NKJ). And again He says, "I am the light of the world. He who follows Me shall not walk in darkness, but have the light of life" (Jn 8:12 NKJ)
- The sun radiates heat. Ever heard of solar energy? Heat represents the Holy Spirit who is our power. John 6:63 says, "It is the Spirit who gives life..." and Acts 1:8 declares, "But you shall receive power when the Holy Spirit has come upon you..."

With that understood, we can answer the question. When we pray, we are praying to the Godhead. If we must have a

57

breakdown, we pray *to* God the Father, ***through*** (in) the name of Jesus Christ, and *by* the leading of the Holy Spirit. God is Creator of all and over all and it's before Him we will stand. Jesus is our passage to God ("no man comes to the Father except through me"). The Holy Spirit empowers us and directs our hearts and minds as we submit to God in prayer. The Holy Spirit "will guide you into all truth" (Jn 16:13), and "helps in our weaknesses for we do not know what we should pray for as we ought, but the Spirit Himself makes intercession for us with groanings which cannot be uttered" (Rom 8:26 NKJ). However, in the same way in which we cannot separate the mass of the sun from its light and its heat, we cannot separate God the Father from the Son and the Holy Spirit.

The bottom line is: God's got it covered when we pray. Frankly, I really don't think God is so concerned with semantics. I don't think He minds if we call Him Father, Jesus, or the Holy Spirit – just as long as we call.

Day 14: Praying to our Triune God

Pray to God the Father, the ever-existent One.

Day 14: Praying to our Triune God (continued)

Pray to God the Son, the Light of the World.

Day 14: Praying to our Triune God

Pray to the Holy Spirit, your power to live this Christian life.

James 5:17-18 says, "Elijah was a man with a nature like ours, and he prayed earnestly that it would not rain; and it did not rain on the land for three years and six months. And he prayed again, and the heaven gave rain, and the earth produced its fruit" (NKJ). Before reading this verse, we probably thought of Elijah as a pretty special person. He was. Elijah was a major prophet. He heard God speaking to him. He went head-up with Jezebel and the 400 prophets of Baal on Mount Carmel and won. He was so amazing that he didn't even have to die. God swept him up in a fiery chariot and took him to Heaven special delivery.

Yet this verse describes Elijah simply as "a man with a nature like ours." Nothing incredible from his life is mentioned. The one action that moved him and moved the hand of God was the fact that "he prayed earnestly." And when he prayed, phenomenal things happened.

Elijah was no different from us at all. He was a regular person. He experienced the same sensations and impressions, was moved by similar passions, and felt identical emotions. Yet he stopped the rain, called down fire from heaven, and rode in a chauffeured limo (okay, a chariot) bound for Glory. How'd he do it? Prayer.

How do we, then, as regular people, experience those same types of amazing feats? It's simple. Catch God's ear through earnest prayer. God listens attentively to regular people. Pray.

Day 15: Regular People Pray and Things Happen

Pray about the out-of-the-ordinary.

Day 15: Regular People Pray and Things Happen (continued)

Sit Beside the Source
Day 16

I remember playing the telephone game as a kid. My friends and I would sit around the room and the first person whispered a message into the ear of the person next to her. Then that person would whisper the message to the next person, and so on. You could say the message only once and you had to pass along exactly what you thought you heard. The last person to receive the message would report it out loud. Inevitably, the final message would be vastly different from the original one. Sometimes the last message was so distorted that it was completely nonsensical and often unintelligible.

We all had a good laugh at how far from the original the final message became. Then we tried to figure out where the message got messed up. The people near the end the chain swore they heard what they heard, while the people near the source of the message insisted they communicated the right thing clearly. All in fun, we pointed out the blame, and then we played our next round, determined to get it right. We never did.

It's possible for this to happen when it comes to the Word of God. When we are not praying and reading the Bible for ourselves, we rely on others to communicate God's message. How do we know they heard it right? There's only one way to know: sit beside the Source. I'm not saying don't go to church, or listen to Christian speakers, or read Christian books. What I am saying is that we should be like the Bereans whom God calls "of noble character" because "they received the message with great eagerness and examined the Scriptures every day to see if what Paul said was true" (Acts 17:11 NIV).

What is God whispering directly into your ear today?

Day 16: Sit Beside the Source

As you speak with God today, take time to listen. Is He telling you to do, say, believe, start, or stop something? Has he directed you to go somewhere? Journal your conversation with God concerning what He's whispering in your ear.

Day 16: Sit Beside the Source (continued)

Somebody Prayed for Me
Day 17

The lyrics of an old spiritual rattled around in my head after I read my Bible this morning. The song says:

- Somebody prayed for me, had me on their mind,
- Took the time to pray for me.
- I'm so glad they prayed, I'm so glad they prayed, I'm so glad they prayed for me.

The song goes on into succeeding verses replacing the word "somebody" with "my mother," "my father," "the preacher," and "my Jesus."

What passage sparked this song to flame in my spirit? Hebrews 7:25-27. It says, "Therefore He is also able to save to the uttermost those who come to God through Him, since *He always lives to make intercession for them*. For such a High Priest was fitting for us, who is holy, harmless, undefiled, separate from sinners, and has become higher than the heavens; who does not need daily, as those high priests, to offer up sacrifices, first for His own sins and then for the people's, for this He did once for all when He offered up Himself" (NKJ, emphasis added).

Yes, I know others here on earth are praying for me, and I'm extremely grateful. Just yesterday, my husband told me he prays for me every day; what an honor and a blessing! An elderly lady at my church – a stalwart saint for many years – touched my heart and made me laugh when she told me, "I pray for you all the time. I'm old, and I can't do much else other than pray anymore, so that's what I do." The 40 women on my prayer team bump into each other at the Throne Room praying for me. My children pray for me.

But oh my goodness, how fabulous it is to know that even if all those people get busy or sick or sleepy or even get mad at me so that they stop praying for me, I know there's One who "always lives to make intercession" for me. His credentials make Him qualified to get God's attention on my behalf. He's "holy, harmless, undefiled, separate from sinners, and has become higher than the heavens." He also doesn't need to take time offering up prayers for Himself first before He starts to pray for me.

Just in case you're not quite sure who this ringer of a pray-er is, go back a few verses in Hebrews chapter 7 and you'll find His identity in verse 22: "…Jesus has become a surety of a better covenant" (NKJ).

Now you understand the source of the song in my heart. Let's sing the last verse together:
- My Jesus prays for me, has me on His mind,
- Takes the time to pray for me.
- I'm so glad He prays, I'm so glad He prays, I'm so glad He prays for me.

Rejoice! He prays for you too!

Day 17: Somebody Prayed for Me

How thankful are you that Jesus is praying for you? Pray to Him about that here. Maybe you'd like to write a poem or a song. You may even want to discuss with Him exactly what it is He is saying to God about you.

Day 17: Somebody Prayed for Me (continued)

The Armor-bearer
Day 18

The word armor-bearer is derived from two Hebrew words. "Keliy" means something prepared, i.e. any apparatus as an implement, utensil, dress, vessel or weapon, instrument, or jewel, that is made; and "nasa'" which means to lift. Therefore, an armor-bearer is someone who lifts something belonging to someone else. In Biblical days, weapons were big and bulky, therefore a soldier would have someone else traveling with him to carry additional armor and weapons he would need for the battle. In 1 Samuel 14:7, Jonathan's armor-bearer was right there with him. "So his armor-bearer said to him, "Do all that is in your heart. Go then; here I am with you, according to your heart" (NKJ).

Nowadays, Christians are fighting a battle and 2 Corinthians 10:4 tells us "the weapons we fight with are not the weapons of the world. On the contrary, they have divine power to demolish strongholds" (NIV). The only defensive weapon described as part of the armor of God in Ephesians 6:17-18 is "… the sword of the Spirit, which is the word of God" which we use by "praying in the Spirit on all occasions with all kinds of prayers and requests. With this in mind, be alert and always keep on praying for all the saints" (NIV). We fight today with the Word of God and with prayer.

An old Sunday School chorus says:
>We are soldiers in the army
>We have to fight, although we have to cry;
>We have to hold up the blood-stained banner.
>We have to hold it up until we die.

Every soldier needs an armor-bearer. I thank God that I have a prayer team of armor-bearers: over forty mighty, Spirit-filled women of God who pray for me and the ministry God has given me on a regular basis. I call them my Power Team. They lift before the Lord that which He has commissioned me to carry into battle. I may be on the front line actually firing the shots, but they are right there with me in the heat of every battle. Without them, my strength and ammunition would quickly deplete.

Are we armor-bearers for one another? Today, determine to become an armor-bearer for other saints of God. Carry their cares to the Lord. Be right there on the front line with them. We need each other.

Day 18: The Armor-bearer

For whom can you function as armor-bearer today? If possible, contact that person and ask them what it is specifically that you can carry for him/her. Now journal here about carrying your friend's armor.

Day 18: The Armor-bearer (continued)

The Call of God

Oswald Chambers said, "To be brought into the zone of the call of God is to be profoundly altered" (My Utmost for His Highest, 1935). Abram received such a call and entered such a zone.

In Genesis 12:1-3, we listen in as God outlines Abram's call to him:

- Now the LORD had said to Abram: "Get out of your country, from your family and from your father's house, to a land that I will show you. I will make you a great nation; I will bless you and make your name great; and you shall be a blessing. I will bless those who bless you, and I will curse him who curses you; and in you all the families of the earth shall be blessed" (NKJ).

What a word! This seven-fold blessing shows us at least three characteristics of God's call to us. First, the call is personal. God spoke directly to Abram. God is perfectly able to get our attention and speak directly to us so that we know it's Him and we are absolutely sure of what He's saying. God personalizes His calls to us, designing them specifically for the person He made us to be.

Second, God's call is pointed. Abram knew exactly what he had to do when he heard God's call. "Get out of your country, from your family and from your father's house, to a land that I will show you." Abram instantly obeyed in three of these four categories. He left his country, left his father's house, and went to the land God showed him, but he didn't leave all his family. He took Lot with him, and later Lot became a lot of trouble. When God calls, He expects us to follow the specific instructions He gives. Although we may not know why at the time, He has His reasons for telling us to do things a particular way, and we can gum up the whole works if we decide to get creative.

Third, God's call is productive. God called Abram in order to see things happen. God had much bigger things in store for Abram than the comfortable life he had in Ur. And what God had in store for Him would further the cause of the Kingdom. In the process of following God's call, Abram himself would also be abundantly blessed. So it is when God announces His call to us. By hearing and obeying His call, we'll see things happen, the Kingdom will be expanded, He will be glorified, and we will be blessed.

Proverbs 1:33 says, "But whoever listens to me will live in safety and be at ease, without fear of harm" (NIV). Indeed, once we hear God's call, we are profoundly altered and immediately thrust into a decision: do we ignore it or do we obey it? We're never the same no matter which choice we make. To ignore God's call might bring immediate relief from the pressure of hearing the call in the first place, but we ultimately doom ourselves to a life that never reaches its full potential of joy or satisfaction. To obey God's call is to open ourselves to endless wonder and glory both in this life and the life to come.

Which will it be for you today?

Day 19: The Call of God

God's call is personal. Journal (to God) about His personal call for you.

God's call is pointed. Pray in writing here about the specific points of God's call for you.

Day 19: The Call of God (continued)

God's call is productive. Journal here about how God would have you be productive as you operate in the call He has given you.

The Fire is Still Burning

Day 20

While reading through Leviticus, all the talk of the sacrifices can get a little tedious and confusing. Bring a bull, bring a lamb, bring a ram, or sacrifice a turtledove. We can sympathize with the priests who had to keep all the rules straight and deal with the killing and blood every day. There was a steady stream of forgiveness-seekers traipsing in and out of the temple to atone for their sins. What a job.

Leviticus 6:13 says, "A fire shall always be burning on the altar; it shall never go out" (NKJ). This one little verse caused me to shift my focus from the priests to the Pardoner. Sure, it cost the sinner the price of his offering, and it cost the priest the time and energy of the ritual, but it cost those animals their very lives, and it ultimately cost God His Son in order to forgive our sins. The "trouble" on our part to come and ask for forgiveness is well overshadowed by God's amazing love to always be there to give it. The fire on the altar always burned, indicating God's open arms of invitation for us to ask for the forgiveness we so desperately need.

The Psalmist says, "Then I acknowledged my sin to you and did not cover up my iniquity. I said, 'I will confess my transgressions to the LORD'-- and you forgave the guilt of my sin. Selah" (Ps 32:5 NIV). The Hebrew word for 'confess' in this verse is 'yadah,' which means "to bemoan by wringing the hands, to cast out." In the New Testament, the Apostle John tells us, "If we confess our sins, He is faithful and just to forgive us our sins and to cleanse us from all unrighteousness" (1 Jn 1:9 NKJ). The Greek word for confess used here is 'homologeo' meaning "to assent or acknowledge."

Unlike Old Testament times, we no longer have to bring bulls, goats, rams, and turtledoves, but we are still required to confess our sins—to acknowledge by being truly sorry and intent on turning away from. When we do so, we will find our loving Father is still "faithful and just to forgive us our sins and to cleanse us from all unrighteousness."

Approach the throne today with true confession. Thank God, the fire is still burning.

Day 20: The Fire is Still Burning

Confess your sins to God. Discuss with Him what specific steps you will take to obey His word.

(For example: Lord, I have dishonored You through my over-eating. Please forgive me and strengthen me to start honoring You in the temple of my body. I will see my doctor this week and take his suggestions for starting a healthy eating plan.)

Day 20: The Fire is Still Burning (continued)

What a Prayer Reflects
Day 21

It's a good idea to write your prayers. Prayers we verbally utter can get lost to us in the atmosphere; they can be said and forgotten. However, prayers we write are fixed in front of us. They capture the essence of moments that can be relived, reviewed, cherished, and remembered. Since we know we can't lie to God, written prayers become a registry of our relationship with Him and a valuable legacy for our children, grand-children, and generations beyond.

1 Chronicles 4:10, a verse nestled and almost hidden in another boring list of "begats," is a sincere prayer of an otherwise obscure historical figure. Even though his mother gave him a negative name, Jabez (which means to grieve or sorrowful) did not allow the circumstances of his birth determine His attitude toward God. He realized "it is what it is" when it came to his life's situation, but focused on God's truth and tomorrow. His prayer is a reflection of an honorable heart toward God.

"And Jabez called on the God of Israel saying, "Oh, that You would bless me indeed, and enlarge my territory, that Your hand would be with me, and that You would keep me from evil, that I may not cause pain!" So God granted him what he requested" (NKJ).

Notice that Jabez's prayer is not void of requests for himself, but it combines those requests with an understanding of God's sovereignty and control. Study each point of the prayer as it could apply to you if you were to pray like this:
- Called on God – Recognize who the God is on whom you are calling, with all His associated attributes

- Bless me indeed –Concentrate on your personal relationship with God. Ask yourself, "Am I part of the family, even in line for the blessings of God?"
- Enlarge my territory – Be about the business ministry. Know that your life influences others.
- Your hand be with me – Submit to God's direction and operate in his favor.
- Keep me from evil – Give attention to personal holiness.
- That I may not cause pain – Conduct your relationships with others in an upright, honest, and loving manner.

Start journaling your prayers and after about a month or so, read back over them. What do your prayers reflect? Does God detect an honorable heart so that He can grant you your requests as He did for Jabez?

Day 21: What a Prayer Reflects

Here is the Prayer of Jabez from 1 Chronicles 4:10 – "And Jabez called on the God of Israel saying, 'Oh, that You would bless me indeed, and enlarge my territory, that Your hand would be with me, and that You would keep *me* from evil, that I may not cause pain!' So God granted him what he requested."

Now pray your own version of Jabez's prayer using the guideline below:

- Call on God:

- Bless me indeed:

- Enlarge my territory

- Your hand be with me:

Day 21: What a Prayer Reflects (continued)

- Keep me from evil:

- That I may not cause pain:

When You Pray

Day 22

Aside from the occasion of blatant disrespect and belittling by an employer, there's nothing worse than an employee who continually insists on repeating, "That's not in my job description." Nowadays, it's a tremendous blessing just to have a job in the first place. Reaching beyond our written contract and helping out for the good of the company or for the relief of a colleague shouldn't be an instance for complaint. In fact, common sense and common decency dictate that some things are just expected of our position and don't need to be expressly written out before we'll submit to performing them.

So it is with prayer and our Christian lives. In Matthew chapter 6, Jesus approached it as a foregone conclusion that we pray ("And when you pray…" v. 5), but realized we needed instruction on how to get prayer right.

First, pray **on your own**. Jesus tells us not to pray like the hypocrites do, loud and with the intention of being seen. Instead, He says, "But you, when you pray, go into your room, and when you have shut your door, pray to your Father who is in the secret place…" (Mat 6:6a NKJ). God actually desires alone time with us, without distractions, and in a place where we can focus on Him (He is already constantly focused on us).

Second, **be original**. Jesus says, "And when you pray, do not use vain repetitions as the heathen do…" (Mat 6:7a NKJ). We shouldn't plagiarize prayer. We're to talk to God about our personal issues, concerns, and desires rather than simply repeating what we've heard others say. God's concerned about what's really on our hearts. We can be honest with Him when we pray.

Third, *be organized*. In Matthew 6:9-13 Jesus gives us a model, on which to hang our prayer thoughts, so that we approach it in the right way. He says, "In this manner, therefore, pray..." In other words, we follow this pattern as we elaborate with our own heart's cries. How can we be organized and original at the same time? Here are some suggestions using the prayer Jesus taught.

"Our Father in heaven, hallowed be Your name." Take time to express adoration of God. Speak to Him of who He is. Bless Him for His attributes.

"Your kingdom come. Your will be done on earth as it is in heaven." Ask for understanding of what God's will is concerning the different things you are praying about. Find Scriptures that relate to those issues.

"Give us this day our daily bread." Talk to God about your specific needs for the day you are facing and express your trust in Him to meet those needs.

"And forgive us our debts, as we forgive our debtors." Speak with God about areas of sinfulness in your life. Ask for His forgiveness and for His instruction and help in turning from those sinful ways. Also speak to God about those to whom you need to extend forgiveness.

"And do not lead us into temptation, but deliver us from the evil one." Be honest with God about the things that tempt you. Ask Him how to avoid those temptations and pray for deliverance from the enemy of your soul who ever seeks to bring you down.

"For Yours is the kingdom and the power and the glory forever. Amen." Close your prayer times reiterating your trust in God and your reliance on His power in and through your life.

Well, what are you waiting for – go somewhere and pray!

Day 22: When You Pray

Now it's your turn. Chronicle your prayer here as you follow Jesus's model prayer.

Express adoration of God.

Ask for understanding of what God's will is.

Day 22: When You Pray (continued)

Talk to God about your specific needs for the day you are facing.

Speak with God about areas of sinfulness in your life.

Day 22: When You Pray (continued)

Be honest with God about the things that tempt you.

Close your prayer times reiterating your trust in God.

Within Reach
Day 23

My desk is set up so that all of my supplies are within easy reach. I can put my hands on my Synonym Finder when it's time for me to make a great outline for a talk. My pens, pencils, highlighters, scissors, and letter opener are in a wire mesh cup to my right next to the small matching bowl of paperclips, and the matching bin for current letters and files. On the left side of the desk are my prayer list box, pencil sharpener, phone, and a plastic bin holding note pads and stamps. Business cards, return address labels, staples, tape, and other oft-used items are in other parts of the desk. The rest of my office isn't very big, so one desk chair swivel and a few steps connect me with all my writing life needs. And now that I'm working from home, my husband, with his sound advice, witty comments, and great cooking is also fortunately close at hand.

Like many other people in the United States right now, I'm at home working at this desk, with everything close by, because the job where I was employed fulltime for the past 17 years went out of business. I can't say, though, that I'm unemployed thanks to someone else who is within reach. Jeremiah 23:23 says, "'Am I a God near at hand,' says the LORD, 'And not a God afar off?'" (NKJ).

The answer to the question is, "Yes, God, You are near at hand; You're not a God who is afar off." The best thing I can have within reach at my desk is my God, my employer. Guess what? He's within your reach too; He's near at hand, not afar off. Whether you work behind a desk at home or from a high rise, at a school or in boardrooms, in front of a camera or behind the scenes – wherever you work, God is within reach. He's the main supply we need.

Day 23: Within Reach

Journal your prayer here about God being close at hand.

Day 23: Within Reach (continued)

(… continued)

You Get What You Come For
Day 24

I attend Christian writers' conferences. At these gatherings, hopeful authors assemble to learn all about writing and the writing life from acquisitions editors, freelancers, agents, manuscript reviewers, and publicists. The editors get the most attention because they have the power to give a thumbs-up to our projects, and launch them into the process toward becoming a published piece.

Simply being in the editors' presence is not enough to reach our publishing goals. We are expected to approach one of them with our proposals. Unless we make that contact, the wheels will not start turning for us. We'll return home with the same ideas with which we arrived, no closer to publication than we were before we spent the money to attend the conference. In order to get what we went for, we had to speak up and take advantage of the reason why the editors were there – to find new projects for their companies to publish.

In Luke 5:17, we find a similar scenario: "Now it happened on a certain day, as He was teaching, that there were Pharisees and teachers of the law sitting by, who had come out of every town of Galilee, Judea, and Jerusalem. And the power of the Lord was present to heal them" (NKJ). The pronoun "them" at the end of that verse refers back to the Pharisees and teachers of the law. God's power was available to make *them* whole. So why then didn't they walk away whole? Another guy, whose friends pushed past some barriers to help him get to Jesus, took advantage of the healing that was initially present that day to heal the Pharisees and the teachers of the law. Although the big shots were in Jesus' presence, they failed to take advantage of the power He had for them because they refused to get involved with Him.

William Carey, a famous missionary to India, had a motto: "Expect great things from God; Attempt great things for God." At every writers' conference I attend, I approach editors pitching new ideas that I fully expect they will love and their houses will publish. Once I get the word of acceptance (a contract) from the publisher, I'm immediately on the move to finish writing that manuscript. I approach God's word every day with that same zeal. I expect to hear amazing things from Him that are vital to my life and that He fully expects me to put into action immediately. And every day, I get what I came for.

Do you expect to receive something from Gods' word every time you read it? You should. And then is your attitude one that is determined to receive what He has for you and put it into action immediately? It should be. You get from God what you come for.

Day 24: You Get What You Come For

Journal here about what you have come to God for.

Day 24: You Get What You Come For

Read a passage of Scripture. Write here what God spoke to your heart from the passage you just read.

Your First Reaction

What's your first reaction when a problem arises? Some of us call somebody – a friend, the pastor, our mother – to talk things through, bounce off ideas, or know someone is on your side. Others turn inward to isolate themselves from the world until the pain or the issue eases up a bit. Some lash out, immediately retorting back whatever that first feeling pulls up from within. Or maybe you handle the dilemma by eating, cursing, shopping, drinking, going to a movie, or taking a long drive. While all of these are mechanisms to let off steam, few if any (especially not the cursing, drinking, and lashing out) solve the problem.

A man in Matthew chapter 17 faced a problem with his child. He approached Jesus and said, "Lord, have mercy on my son, for he is an epileptic and suffers severely; for he often falls into the fire and often into the water. So I brought him to Your disciples, but they could not cure him" (Mat 17:15 NKJ). After chastising the disciples for their unbelief, Jesus instructed the man saying, "Bring him here to Me" (verse 17b) and he rebuked the demon so that the child was cured. Jesus went on to say that this type would come out only by prayer and fasting (verse 21).

It struck me that this man's first reaction was to take his son to the disciples rather than to Jesus. All through the Gospels, we read of the flocking multitudes taking their sick to Jesus, but this guy took his son to the disciples first. We do know that the disciples healed people and cast out demons to their own surprise when Jesus sent them out to do so (see Lk 10:17), and that's the point. While Jesus was with them, the focus was on Him, not on them. The disciples could do nothing without directly being sent by Jesus to do so, and whatever miraculous things they did always turned the attention back to Jesus, the source of the miraculous.

Our first reaction in any difficulty, crisis, or predicament needs to be to look to Jesus. He personally invites us to do just that. "Come to Me, all *you* who labor and are heavy laden, and I will give you rest. Take My yoke upon you and learn from Me, for I am gentle and lowly in heart, and you will find rest for your souls. For My yoke *is* easy and My burden is light" (Mat 11:28-30 NKJ).

Next time you face a problem, try Jesus first. You can always go back to your other responses if turning to Jesus first doesn't work. What have you got to lose? But I'm confident you'll find that taking your burdens to the Lord will be the best decision.

Day 25: Your First Reaction

What problem, issue, thought, or concern have you taken everywhere except to the Lord? Use these pages to change that. Take that particular burden to the Lord now.

Day 25: Your First Reaction (continued)

Your Heart's Desire
Day 26

While I was attending Emmanuel Community Church in Gardena, CA some years ago, my pastor, Pastor Frederick Holmes, asked me the question, "What do you want from life?" Without hesitation I answered, "I want my life to count." That short conversation became a defining moment in my life wherein I had put into words the theme of my own existence, the thing that makes me "tick," my heart's desire.

It didn't take much thought after those first six words to realize that my life could only have lasting worth as I bonded my desire for myself with God's desires for me. I figure it this way: If I am following the Lord daily, whatever I do will be His desire for me to do, and the outcome will have lasting value that matters in the grand scheme of things. The ultimate result? My life will have counted. Vineyard's praise song, *Cry of my Heart*, reflects what I mean. The chorus simply says:

> It is the cry of my heart to follow You,
> It is the cry of my heart to be close to You,
> It is the cry of my heart to follow,
> All of the days of my life

What is your heart's desire? Is it something God would have for you? Is it something that, if fulfilled, you could proudly lay at Jesus'
feet as an offering to Him? With the preceding thoughts in mind, The Psalmist's prayer is also mine for you today: "May He grant you according to your heart's *desire,* and fulfill all your purpose" (Ps 20:4 NKJ).

Day 26: Your Heart's Desire

How would you answer my pastor's question, "What do you want out of life?" What is your heart's desire?

Day 26: Your Heart's Desire (continued)

My Prayer Box
Day 27

I have a lot of people to pray for and things to do. In order to get everyone on my prayer list prayed for and everything on my to-do list done, I had to figure out a system. I amaze my friends by how much I can get done in the same 24-hour period they have, and I do so by dividing my chores into bite-sized pieces. Piece by piece, lots of things can be accomplished. My prayer list is divided the same way.

Years ago, I started using my prayer box. My box holds 3-by-5 index cards and 7 dividers. The dividers are labeled as follows: Me, James, Children, Ministries, Single Christians, Christian Marriages, The Unsaved. Behind each divider are cards on which I write specific prayer needs. Each of our children and grandchildren has his/her own card, and it's the same for each ministry, single friend, and family. The unsaved are merely listed by name because the only thing I pray for them is that they receive salvation. On Monday, I pray for myself and my husband James, Tuesday is dedicated to the children, and so on through the week. This way, I cover everyone within the week, spend quality time in prayer, and still get other things done throughout the day.

Now don't get me wrong; I also pray for people throughout the day and even on days that are not specifically set aside for them. For example, whenever I'm driving and I see cars like the ones driven by our children, I pray for them. So when I see a Chrysler 300, I pray for Lori; or when a Dodge Charger whizzes by, prayers go up for Mark, and so on. My box helps me remember all the important issues. It also serves as a praise reminder, because I can look back over the years and see how God has always faithfully answered.

Unlike me, God needs no special reminders to keep our concerns before Him. He knows and cares about everything we go through. Psalm 56:8 says, "You number my wanderings; Put my tears into Your bottle; *Are they* not in Your book?" (NKJ) What a blessing and comfort to know that God is looking over us, looking out for us, looking to be right there with us when we hurt – close enough to catch our tears. His deep care for us should move us to care deeply for others. Maybe we can't catch each other's tears in bottles, but we can catch each other's concerns in a box. May we care for others as God has cared for us.

Day 27: My Prayer Box

List by categories all the people and issues for which you need to pray. Think about how you could separate this list so you can spend quality time praying for just one part of the list every day.

Day 27: My Prayer Box (continued)

Confident Prayer

Day 28

It's easy to ask when we know our requests are going to be granted. You know the feeling. You'd been good all week, so when you asked for that ice cream cone on Saturday, Mom said, "Of course!" You worked hard through school posting A's on your transcript, so when you applied for your first choice college, the admissions office sent back a letter that said, "Congratulations, you're in!" She stole your heart and you promised her a future of romance and laughter even through the hard times, so on bended knee you proposed and she said, "Yes!" The finance department ran your credit and the manager is saying, "You can head over to the realtor to pick up your keys. The house is yours." Sweet!

Yes, asking is easy when our ducks are in a row. We can approach with confidence the holder of the blessing. I John 5:14-15 says, "Now this is the confidence that we have in Him, that if we ask anything according to His will, He hears us. And if we know that He hears us, whatever we ask, we know that we have the petitions that we have asked of Him" (NKJ). The Greek word for "confidence" used here is "parrhesia" (par-rhay-see'-ah) and it means "all outspokenness, frankness, bluntness, and being openly assured." Therefore, in bold assurance, I can take to the bank the fact that God hears me and grants the petitions I am asking of Him.

But wait: that assurance does come with one tiny little caveat. We have our ducks in a row when we ask "according to His will." In other words, the sovereign God still holds the cards. We exist to serve Him, not the other way around. So when we ask for things that are not in line with His will, He is under no obligation to grant those to us. The bold confidence in our asking comes only when we are requesting that which is already a part of His will for our lives.

How do we know what's already a part of His will for our lives? By being in constant communion with Him. The better I know the Savior, the more in tune with Him I become. I wouldn't then dare ask Him to do anything for me that's outside of His character. Confident prayer rests in our relationship with the Master. Strong ties; sure requests and answers.

Day 28: Confident Prayer

Have you been praying about anything that you are not very confident about? Or maybe you have neglected to approach God with a certain request because you're not quite sure it's in His will to grant you that request. Go to God here about such issues. As you talk with Him, let Him direct you to Scriptures that will help your confidence to either keep asking or stop asking.

Day 28: Confident Prayer (continued)

Last Resort Praying

Day 29

The woman with the issue of blood (Mark 5:25-34) is a perfect example of someone who tried everything at her disposal to overcome her problem before she approached Jesus for help. The scripture passage tells us that she "had a flow of blood for twelve years, and had suffered many things from many physicians. She had spent all that she had and was no better, but rather grew worse" (verses 25 and 26). Mind you, nothing in the story indicates she had shunned Jesus' help in the first place. The story simply gives us the facts of her case. For twelve years she had suffered from her condition, and for twelve years, she had tried to find a cure.

When the woman heard that Jesus was in the vicinity, she was in the perfect frame of mind to receive. First, she was looking for help. Then she heard that the healing Man would be in town. She expected Jesus to make the distinctive difference she needed, and she reached out to touch the hem of His robe.

Perhaps you are at a point where Jesus is your last resort. You've tried everything else, and maybe you've even spent lots of money doing so. Follow the path of the woman with the issue of blood.

- Don't give up. Continue to look for help.
- Know that the healing Man is in town. Jesus is ever present to meet you at the point of your need.
- Expect for Him to make the distinctive difference in your situation that you need.
- Reach out and touch Him. This is simply accomplished through prayer.

What was the outcome for the woman? As soon as she touched the hem of Jesus' garment, we read, "Immediately the fountain of her blood was dried up, and she felt in her body that she was

119

healed of the affliction. And Jesus, immediately knowing in Himself that power had gone out of Him, turned around in the crowd and said, 'Who touched My clothes?'...And He looked around to see her who had done this thing... And He said to her, 'Daughter, your faith has made you well. Go in peace, and be healed of your affliction'" (verses 29-34, NKJ).

Besides desperation, last resort praying involves touch. Sometimes we don't realize our need for Jesus until we've exhausted all other avenues. That's okay; He'll wait. You'll wear yourself out before you wear out His patience. Reach out and touch the Master's robe today. Help still flows from it.

Day 29: Last Resort Praying

Do you have an "issue of blood" type problem; something you've been dealing with unsuccessfully for many years? Maybe you struggle with over-eating or overspending so that your weight or poor financial condition are out of whack. Perhaps you smoke, drink, or do drugs (over-the-counter or illegal). You may have trouble controlling your anger, your mouth, or your time. Journal today about the lingering problems you are now willing to take to Jesus, touch His garment, and be healed of.

Day 29: Last Resort Praying (continued)

When it Really Matters
Day 30

When one of our sons entered his last year of college, he found himself owing money to the school which had to be paid before he could register. Because of some of his other financial obligations, he was short. When he expressed his problem to us, I was ready to front him the money; after all, he had only this one more year to go. However, his dad felt he needed to tough his way through, so as we discussed the situation, he ended his comments to me by saying, "And don't you help him."

I was crushed. All I could see was my child's three years of hard work flying out the window because of a few hundred dollars. Was this lesson really that important? Still, despite my love for my son, I was under scriptural obligation to respect my husband's wishes. All that was left for me to do was pray.

And pray I did. I visited my son's church with him the following Sunday. At prayer time during the service, congregants were invited to the altar to pray. I grabbed my boy by the hand and headed up to the front. Together we knelt and I cried out to God. Since I'm generally not prone to crying, I even surprised myself by how ardently the words and tears flowed. This really mattered and I knew only God could help.

1 Peter 5:6-7 says, "Therefore humble yourselves under the mighty hand of God, that He may exalt you in due time, casting all your care upon Him, for He cares for you" (NKJ). I saw this verse spring to life the very next day. My son called me from school and said, "Mom, I'm enrolled." He had figured out a way to decrease his food allowance, thus netting him enough funds in his school account to satisfy the previous semester's debt.

All entities were satisfied. Our son got into school for his senior year, learned a valuable financial lesson, and boosted his confidence in himself. My husband stood his ground, letting our son see the importance of better financial planning. And I respected my husband's wishes and increased my faith in the God who cares about what really matters to me.

When facing an issue that really matters – when we find ourselves between the proverbial rock and a hard place – we need to remember I Peter 5:6-7. Let's humble ourselves under God's mighty hand, believing for His exaltation at just the right time, and standing strong because He really does care about the things which concern us.

Day 30: When it Really Matters

What really matters to you today? Pour out your heart to God. Humble yourself under His mighty hand, knowing that He cares for you and will exalt you at just the right time.

Day 30: When it Really Matters (continued)

Even the Little Things

Day 31

Not long ago, my husband purchased a classic car, the kind he's wanted for years. The car was clearly a project for his retired years. To get things started, he needed to have it towed from its present location to a dealership that specialized in that kind of automobile. As we triumphantly drove away from the sale, he said to me, "Now we need a tow truck."

Right then and there, I called out a simple little prayer, "God, we need a tow truck." We drove about another half block and I said, "Honey, your friend's tuxedo shop is just around the corner. Since he's worked in this neighborhood for some time, perhaps he knows someone who can help us."

We pulled into the shopping center, parked, and entered the shop. Although my husband's friend wasn't there, his apprentice was. We shared our dilemma with him and to our amazement he said, "Man, all I hang out with are tow truck guys. I even know of the perfect shop that specializes in just that kind of vehicle."

I thought, *Wow, God. You answer even little prayers like that?* Then Luke 12:6-7a came to mind. It says, "What's the price of two or three pet canaries? Some loose change, right? But God never overlooks a single one. And he pays even greater attention to you, down to the last detail—even numbering the hairs on your head!" (The Message: The Bible in Contemporary Language)

God cares about every detail of our lives, even the little things. Don't be afraid to talk to God about everything.

Day 31: Even the Little Things

What are the little things you'd like to share with God? Feel free to do so here.

Day 31: Even the Little Things (continued)

www.ingramcontent.com/pod-product-compliance
Lightning Source LLC
Chambersburg PA
CBHW072026040426
42447CB00009B/1752